Mind Song

To: David
Congratulations!
From: Grove United
Methodist Church
June 2, 1985

MIND SONG

Donna Swanson

The Upper Room
Nashville, Tennessee

MIND SONG

Copyright © 1978 by Donna Swanson

All rights reserved.
No part of this book may be reproduced in any manner whatsoever without written permission of the publisher except in brief quotations embodied in critical articles or reviews. For information address The Upper Room, 1908 Grand Avenue, Nashville, Tennessee 37203.

First printing: June 1978 (8)

ISBN 0-8358-0364-3

Printed in the United States of America

Mind Song
is
*lovingly dedicated
to those fellow pilgrims
who believed
I had a song worth singing*

Contents

Foreword   9

Preface   11

Poet and Pilgrim   17

Seeker and Scribe   45

Woman and Wayfarer   67

Index of Titles   96

Foreword

Poets are peculiar people. They often have the capacity to see events, hear sounds, and feel feelings that many of us miss. Novelist John Galsworthy speaks of "the significant trifle" as the key to good writing—the little, unimportant, commonplace details that convey a mood, a feeling, an event, a personality, or a relationship. I think the ability to capture the significant trifle is what makes a good poet.

Donna Swanson has that kind of ability. She and I have been friends through our letters for many years, and she has shared her poetry with me regularly. Not being a poet myself, I cannot evaluate her poetry professionally. But I can say that Donna's writings have frequently helped me to see God more clearly, myself more realistically, my neighbor more sympathetically, and life, with all its mystery, more enthusiastically.

For centuries, God has been speaking to us about life, the nature of his love, and our human needs through the work of the psalmists and poets. I'm grateful that he continues to do so today through poets like Donna Swanson.

Bruce Larson

Preface

During the time in which the poetry in *Mind Song* was written, I was struggling to become whole. I could not understand at that time what wholeness was, only that it was not me. I felt scattered and shattered into a multiplicity of personalities. None of them was violent or psychotic, simply going in different directions, as though my life were many rivers. Now, as I look back, I can see that what was struggling to be was that unique creation of God who was the real Donna Swanson.

I can remember as a child feeling free and alive and capable of all the dreams and visions with which my head was filled. But I also remember "learning" that it was foolish to believe in myself, "learning" there were limits beyond which one could not go without an education. I remember "learning" that people laughed at imagination and were suspicious of originality. All children go through this. It's called "growing up and becoming sensible." We have mistakenly equated it with "putting away childish things." And I put away childish things. I put them away so deep I didn't recognize them when they began to beg for recognition as my true self.

So light and wistful was that voice from my heart! So hard to hear! It whispered in my paintings at first. There was a time when I believed painting would be enough for it. When the act of creating on canvas a world of my own, a world through which I could communicate, even though I did not know *what* I wanted to communicate, seemed the release I needed. And I enjoyed the painting. I even became somewhat proficient at it.

But there came a time when it was not enough. My children were demanding more and more of my time. There was really no market in a farming community for paintings, and beneath it all, that voice was growing stronger. "Listen to me!" it begged. But I pushed it away, because I was afraid of what it might tell me to do or to be. It was easy to ignore it when my family obligations were so heavy. And church work was always there to make me believe I was doing God's will. I took up handcrafts, which were easier to do in short time periods. And I became good at that, too. Not an expert, but good. And still the emptiness echoed within the corridors of my mind. How patient God was! Never letting me go! Always beckoning to me through the hollow places of my soul!

I can't remember when words became so important. I've always loved to "play" with words. I liked tests in school because it was fun to figure out the answers by the wording of the questions. I immediately fell in love with "The Highwayman," "Rime of the Ancient Mariner," and the poems of Edgar Allen Poe. I delighted in the rhythm of the words and the vivid descriptions and mind images they contained. I picked up straight A's in history, because my answers were so long and complicated the teacher got tired of reading them! But never during all that time did I aspire to be a writer or ever dream that one day I would be painting pictures with words rather than brushes.

Then, gradually, the tension increased. My world shrank to eight rooms with wall-to-wall children, toys, and responsibilities, and no time for thinking or being. I knew I loved my children. I enjoyed them and felt fulfilled as I watched them go through the baby stages and become persons. But why at the same time did I so resent their monopolizing my time? Was something terribly wrong with me? Was I an unfit mother? A freak who resented the time and attention they demanded?

I called Doug Dickey, a family friend and minister, and asked to talk with him. As he listened to the classic symptoms of the "trapped housewife syndrome" he gave no indication that my story was so familiar. But then, he didn't give me a lecture or a lot of pat answers, either.

Instead, he gave me a book by D. Elton Trueblood entitled *The Philosophy of Religion,* and told me to take it home and read it. For two weeks I struggled through that book with an encyclopedic dictionary at my elbow. Not having been to college, I knew nothing of the philosophic terms. "Dialectical materialism" and "theistic realism" might have been dissertations on Martian farming for all I knew! And I still don't have them all straight. But what I did have when I finished that beautiful book was a new and astonishing sense of God and his plan for the world. I went back to Doug with the words still singing through my mind and asked for more. And, for the next few years, his library became a living spring. More Trueblood, Miller, Lewis, Thielicke, Tillich, and a guy named Bruce Larson.

Oh, I'm not saying I became whole at that time. Far from it. What I became was frustrated and restless and filled with a desperate yearning to be a part of what I was reading. To become one with that larger, truer world of the mind. And that's where it was. The mind. The "real" Donna Swanson still washed dishes, changed diapers, taught Sunday school class, and hoed the garden. But there was another Donna Swanson growing deep in the seclusion of my soul. And that Donna Swanson was growing meddlesome! She insisted that all was not as it should be in my world. And she kept insisting that I seek help.

In this way, I came to the point of going through analysis with a Christian psychologist named Wallace Denton. And it was just before and during this time that the poetry came fully to the surface. As I faced the hurting places deep within, words flowed from my pen like tears. Sometimes they were tears of sorrow and sometimes tears of joy, wonder, and awe of a God so immense. But they were silent words. Words on paper. At first words only for my eyes and perhaps those of Dr. Denton. And somehow, that wasn't enough either.

As I read of the books that told of a new song for the church, I knew I wanted to be a part of that. So, when a book touched me I would write to the author and say so, and perhaps enclose a poem or two indicating where I was in my own pilgrimage. And they wrote back! Not only could I touch on paper, I could be touched back! And they didn't know the Donna Swanson who didn't do all things well, who goofed up the housework and ate too much and all the rest. They just knew the free spirit who wrote words that sang of living and loving and hurting.

This was a whole different dimension of my life. Here, on paper, I could be the Donna Swanson of my childhood, without apology, without self-consciousness. I was free to say and be the best that was within myself. The correspondence narrowed to only a few as Dr. Trueblood, John Killinger, and Charlie Shed gave me words of encouragement. John told me of a new magazine, *alive now*! out of Nashville, and through that was launched a new career with poetry being published and new challenges ahead. It was Bruce Larson, however, who bore the brunt of my struggle with the two Donnas.

But still it was all on paper. I never thought of the two Donna Swansons as the same person. I still could not keep in my mind the thought of people reading and talking about my poetry in places like Nashville or New York or California. There was an unreal quality to that self, as though she were manufactured on my typewriter and lived only at the mercy of the post office.

Then, the poem "Minnie Remembers" took off. One day a person named Kay Henderson called on the telephone and asked to make a film of "Minnie Remembers." She was not calling the "real" Donna, you know, she was calling the paper Donna! And that Donna answered the phone and said, "Yes!" and made arrangements for a trip to Nashville to see her creation filmed. And, oh, what a frightened paper person rode eleven hours on a Greyhound bus to Nashville! She met John Killinger there, she was made a part of the team filming "Minnie," and all the time she kept wondering, "What am I doing here? Who am I that these people value my words?" And she pushed the answer away because it was too scary. But the voice deep inside was getting louder. *"Listen* to me!" And the paper Donna was beginning to move and act and exist.

When *Mind Song* was accepted for publication, there

were more meetings and more people. I encountered Janice Grana and Maxie Dunnam who had known of me and my words even before I knew their names! They knew there was a Donna Swanson who lived in Indiana and who wrote words that painted pictures in the mind, and they loved her! And there were people who wanted to meet her when she came to Nashville! And the voice said, "See! I am real! I am more real than anything you have ever been!"

And all through those years of formation Bruce had been telling me over and over, "You are unique! You are an evangelist! And you are more even than all of that!" But that was only a paper person. He didn't know the "real" Donna. If he did maybe he wouldn't like her. Maybe he would turn away. Slowly, I began to share my doubts with him. I began to let the real me leak through the words. And he didn't turn away! And, later, when we met in person, he affirmed my totality with a beautiful smile and a warm hug. And neither did the people and friends around home turn away as I began to trust them with the paper Donna. Gradually I was able to be known as Donna Swanson, author and poet, as well as Donna Swanson, wife and mother. I learned to play the guitar and my words combined with music so that they not only satisfied my soul in new ways, but they were capable of being shared with others in ways I never imagined.

When "Minnie Remembers" was released as a film, I began showing it at different churches along with a program of music and poetry. And another transformation occurred. Now, I could read the poetry with the same emotion with which it had been written! The paper Donna was speaking and singing and expressing herself! She was real. And she was not paper! She was the most basic expression of my personality! And that basic expression loved her children and her husband and her home with all the beauty of the words within her. The hollow was suddenly flooded with the reality of a wholeness beyond explanation. For the poet and the person were one.

And where was God during this time? Why, God was in Doug and Wallace and Bruce and John Killinger and

John, Melynda, Melyssa, Melanie, and Mac Swanson! He was in Janice and Maxie and Kay and so many beautiful people who called forth the struggling Donna Swanson. He was the ground of my being—the Heaven of my reaching.

Such is the land of *Mind Song*. It is a land of beginning. A song of tomorrow sung from the cool valleys of the past.

Donna Swanson

Poet & Pilgrim

Mind Song

My mind is singing
*   singing*
*   singing*
Joy and sorrow, laughter, tears.
Hoping
seeking
praying
singing
crying, loving through the years.

Mind song moving
*   living*
*   giving*
filling up the empty spaces:
Spinning out the common traces
*   people*
*   places*
*   words and faces!*

Mind song calling, beckoning onward
from the past, the future bringing.
From the hand of sorrow taking
*   molding*
*   shaping*
*   ever making*
songs of praise and gifts of love!

Mind song. That's what it is, you know. To the poet, words are like music running through the mind. No amount of instruction can put that music inside your head. But you can learn to hear it. You can accustom yourself to the lilt of the words until the music begins.

It is not mindless music. Though it finds its counterpoint in the soft whisperings of the wind and the inarticulate sighings of the soul, it is not mindless. For, in the poet, God brings together the gift of music and the gift of intellect, there combining the two in the soul-satisfying gift of poetry.

Mind song. A song that flickers from joy to sorrow; from wonder, to awe, to a restless searching. Not in a tidy progression from darkness to light, but in a dance of life where sunshine and shadow lie intermingled until we move from light to light through shadows of defeat, despair, and sorrow. And the light grows brighter beyond each shadow. Joy takes on a sweeter glow for knowing sorrow. And always God is there . . . calling, beckoning onward.

Words

I am my words.
This shell that conceals my inner being
turns you away.

You see me,
but you don't perceive me.
I stand before you in isolation,
for my spirit is alone.

How my spirit longs
to run unbound!
How I would sing for you
if I were free!

We speak
and our words clash and clatter away
like brittle leaves in winter.

In despair I take up my pen,
unloose the bindings of my soul,
and commune with you
in the only way I know.

The song that was stilled
by prejudice and fear
tumbles from my paper lips
and fills the page with music.

Take my words and love them,
for they are me.

To Be One

To be one,
  whole within myself.
    To know that what I am
      and what I do
springs forth
  from an inner cohesion
    of the soul.

This fledgling
  has manifested itself;
    has struggled to the rim
      of consciousness
and there hung trembling
  on the brink
    of a surer reality.

So weak and fragile
  was its beginning!
    As though the gentlest
      of breezes
was rustling through
  the echoing corridors
    of my mind.

Sleepily the tiny being
  rouses itself,
    surveys the landscape
      of my soul
and, finding it habitable,
  curls itself into the nest
    of my desiring.

Through the years of growing
  the wistful self
    lies almost quiescent;
      with only the faintest stirrings;
until the time
  when, searching unaware,
    I sense its presence.

Shy as a new lover,
 it sings to me,
  woos my seeking heart,
   and guides my wayward thoughts—
Even though I deny
 its existence
  and turn from its leading.

Now, full grown,
 the vibrant life
  within life
   strides forth,
embraces my soul,
 affirms my authenticity,
  and becomes myself!

And I stand whole,
 complete within my many selves,
  unique in my variety,
   ready to move into my destiny!
Welcome, gentle stranger!
 The world has been
  waiting for you!

Dichotomy

There has never been an easy contentment with "life in a box." But it has not been until the last few years that I have begun to feel the value of my gifts as an intrinsic part of my own being. They were always something to be bartered for recognition or acceptance; a barrier to erect behind which I could hide the soiled, rejectable self.

I delight in the rhythm of words and the cadence of thought, but it has been much harder for me to become attuned to the physical side of life. Part of me has always looked askance at the sensuousness of feeling; as though I were not supposed to enjoy the velvet-furred cat twining around my bare legs as I hung out clothes in the apple-sweet tang of autumn. As though, somehow, God wasn't there when I made love to my husband, or when I was moved during a drive home through the ever changing silhouettes of twilight. Or when I enjoyed with childish delight the little brown wren as she engaged in a singing duel with my typewriter.

All the while my religion was teaching me to "crucify" the old me, my viscera were reacting to the world around me with piercing clarity. And because I could not conform to the "pious" image held before me, I rebelled at the institutional church. I began to look for answers beyond the confines of my particular denomination, rather than seeking proofs for a sectarian tradition.

And, as I searched, I discovered a God who had created me whole and complete and who blessed all parts of my being equally: the mystical, the spiritual, and the physical!

Little Turtle

Little turtle,
who has turned you upside down?
Did you come into the open once too often?
Did life find you out?

Did you develop
an appetite for butterflies?
Had ants and bugs
become too ordinary?

Why did you believe, little turtle?
Why did you trust?
Of course it was dark inside!
But it was safe.
Life in the open
is fraught with danger.
Hawks share the sky with butterflies.

Too late, little turtle,
you have been seen.
The sun has dazzled you, and
your dark shell lies vulnerable
before the adventure of light.

Freedom

Sometimes I feel like the pair of mallard ducks my little boy and I tried to drive to the pond in our pasture this morning. They had been hatched under an old hen and raised in the hen run all winter. Now they resisted us at every step and tried vainly to return to the safety of the enclosure. I kept telling Mac how much they would enjoy the water, but even when they were settled in the marsh, their heads would swivel toward the faint cluckings behind. And little more than an hour later they were back waddling along the fence trying to re-enter the "womb" of their beginning.

How like them we are! So afraid to dare the freedom God offers us that we retreat into the safety of traditions that stifle and deform our uniqueness.

Flight

*I stand upon the threshold,
and my new self
laughs with delight
at the prospects before me.*

*I stand upon the threshold
and my old self
whispers dire warnings
of disillusionment.*

*Ah, but I know!
The self that cowered before life
was but a travesty of life.
Far better to have loved!*

*My shell lies scattered.
The nest has blown away
in the winds of change
and the dove must fly.*

*The air is sweet
and the sunlight is dazzling
as on trembling wings
I look down upon the treetops.*

*There was shelter there
and sweet showers.
Others fed me and nurtured me.
It might prove lonely up here.*

*What if my wings should break?
There are other fledglings in the nest now.
And they look to me for food.
Give me soft wings of iron, Father!*

*Plant the wonder of this gift
deep in my soul
that it may produce food
for the fledglings.*

*Turn my thoughts outward
   away from these hurts—
   both real and imagined—
   of long ago.*

*I would fly free
   on wings that glisten
   and move in rhythm
   to your heartbeat.*

*And yet I would be bound
   by silken cords of love
   to the hearts of my brothers and sisters,
   that I might give them words
   for their own songs!*

Challenge

Schweitzer believed that one of our main roles as God's children is to thank him for his creation. That things did not exist for God except through our appreciation of and thankfulness for them. If this is so, what a monumental task lies before us! One glance through my study window dazzles the mind with infinite variety. A yellow butterfly drifts past; lilacs fill the air with fragrance while the apple blossoms create a summer snowfall. John's tractor grumbles in the back forty, and the sturdy black calves lift their faces to be licked clean by the soft-eyed cows.

The struggle to express the images which appear on my mind screen becomes monumental at times. It's like trying to frame the sparkle of soap bubbles. The glimpses are so fleeting and come at the most inopportune times.

To reproduce a picture with words. To express a thought so clearly it sings in the minds of those who read it. To woo and beckon until the one who reads is drawn irresistibly into the adventure of life!

To say to the world, "See! Hear! Experience! And live life with all the uniqueness with which you were created!" To labor to share with others the infinite variety of the ordinary. To see with new eyes the mornings and evenings of life. To walk valleys I've never seen and climb mountains no mortal foot has touched. To be continually and wonderingly born again with each new moment.

So much wonder. So much to be thankful for. Sometimes I am overwhelmed—so full of the need to share my joy with others that the brush or pen seems cold and inadequate in the face of such beauty.

Earth Song

The world is still now.
I wait in that deceptive silence
that may or may not precede the muse.

The world is still
with that hushed awareness
of unconquerable life
waiting to cover the naked bones of winter
with voluptuous reproduction.

Winter hangs trembling
from the tip of a greening elm;
the fleeting rainbow of ice and snow
captured in the purity of a raindrop.

The rich, black trunks make their last stand
before the misty green onslaught;
standing tall and solemn
amid the flamboyant courtship of spring,
lest they be caught dancing unawares.

My hands ache for a brush.
But who can capture this magic?
What artist can take the very breath of God
and lay it on canvas?

Joy

*Joy came walking on silent feet
surprising my heart with its
    laughter.*

*It danced in the eyes of my children
and spilled from the heart of my
    husband.*

*While weary with the pilgrimage
through a dark and lonely country,
I found it as a rippling, curling
    stream
running lightly over the troubled
    stones.*

*And I knew, as I sensed its fullness,
that here was the laughter
    of God.*

Hollow Place

Within each heart there is a hollow place. For some that place is small and comfortable, for others it seems to fill the whole being. Some fill the hollow with self-indulgence, some with education and the quest for knowledge. Others try to drown it with drugs or sex or liquor. But none of these measures fills up the hollow. Some are not content with easy answers or traditional ritual. Pat answers leave questions ringing in the hollow place, and they find themselves restless once more. And in those saner moments when they are aware of their deepest needs, the hollow opens wide and lonely, and they toss on their pillows of convenience.

Even those of us who recognize that hollow place as the longing for communion with God find ourselves trying to fill it with unessential things. We may be called "creative people" who are thought to have an extra measure of what it takes to think up new ideas and new ways of expression. But when we are honest, we know that our "creations" are simply a striving to fill the hollow place. If we can name the shape of God, we can fit him into it.

But God refuses to fit. He keeps moving out ahead, ever beckoning, ever coaxing us on until we fill our pages with questings and longings. It is not a lonely questing, however, for God is there. And ultimately we know he is not angered by our searching, but, indeed, encourages it. For, from our seeking comes a new awareness of him, and maybe those who read our words will sense that shape within themselves and recognize it as their own hollow place.

The Pine

I am a tree uprooted;
 a tall pine who could not bend
 and so I fell,
 and, in my falling,
 tore branch and limb
 from the forest around me.

"Stay my fall!" I cried.
"Teach me to bend, I beg you!"
But my heart is pine.
Lofty and stiff are my branches
 and my unbending heart weeps alone.

I lie here now
 on the softened needles of my defenses.
Feeling the ache of brokenness,
 the agony of imperfection,
 gazing at the sky I scorned.

My roots are cut off from the earth.
They rise above me, naked and exposed.
I cannot plunge them back into
 the soil of my beginnings.
The earth disdains them.

Will I be left here to decay?
Or with what shall my brokenness be healed?
Oh, Carpenter!
Am I to be fashioned for some further use?

Healing

I asked for healing
  but hid the wound.
I cried for mercy
  but would not accept it.

I asked for freedom
  but remained in my safe prison.
I asked for life
  but brooded over death.

God made no demands;
  I supplied my own.
God made no judgements;
  I condemned myself.

Then came one who held
  the gift of healing.
With relentless gentleness
  he flung wide the windows of my soul
  and revealed my prison for what it was.

How beautiful to be caught
  in the hands of God!
To stand unafraid
  in my humanity.

Now love flows freely
  following the cleared channel;
  from God to me
  and to my world!

Empty Spaces

Our world is filled with a myriad of things. No king who lived in olden times, for all his wealth and power, could boast such a life as ours. When we are not working we are moments away from leisure-time activities that would boggle the mind of King Solomon.

Where then are the empty spaces? When do we have time to think on the basic values of life? The merry-go-round whirls faster and faster until we despair of thought. We vow to jump off after just one more ride, to walk away from the world of illusion for a better perspective. But there are bills to be paid, friends to cultivate, once-in-a-lifetime opportunities we just can't afford to miss.

Then, suddenly the music stops. The machinery grinds to a halt, and we stand dazed before the jumbled wreckage of our hopes and dreams. A loved one dies. Our worldly goods disappear. We stand like a frightened Don Quixote before the windmills of life. These are the empty spaces. These are the times when truth stands clear and strong if we will but search for it. And there is One who stands with us in those empty spaces; who stands and waits for us to know him.

Solace

When there are no words
    deep enough
    or clear enough
to reach the hurting of my mind;
When there is no light
    warm enough
    or bright enough
to reach the prison of my soul;
Then do my tears
    seek the solace of God.
When the light of my world
    is darkness
and the singing of words
    echoes in the silence
    like clanging cymbals;
Then do my tears
    fall into the hands of God,
    and there become
the waters of life.
For, brushing away the darkness,
he pours the tears on my heart
and quickens to life the words
    of hope
    and compassion
    and love.
With eyes washed clear
    for seeing,
with hands emptied
    for reaching,
I turn again to the world.

Friend

Friend,
 my soul was heavy,
 for I'd walked a lonely road
 and I was tired.

Then we met,
 and you offered your hand
 in loving acceptance.

I'm sorry I missed seeing
 you for so long;
 that your face was lost in the dark.

But now, my eyes are open,
 and I can see and know
 the wonder of friendship.

You have shown me
 that to be fully human, fully alive,
 is to be loving.

And, with all I am
 at this moment,
 I accept your gift freely.

Be patient, friend,
 for this road is new
 and disturbingly open.

And if I falter
 and seek to draw a shell
 once more around my soul,

Remind me quickly
 how much there is to lose;
 how much to gain.

*Then, someday, somehow,
 I'll find a way to give myself,
 and I'll be whole.*

*Free to be loved;
 free to love,
 a credit to your
 compassion.*

In the Woods

I can hear the spring wind building before I feel the freshening breeze upon my face. It stirs the trees in the orchard and sends before itself a million soft sighings. And, as it passes on, I sit in the calm once again even as I hear it moving on to ruffle yet another tree-clad hillside.

I feel the wind, I hear it, but I don't know its origin or its destination. Why, then, must I labor so diligently to understand God's Spirit which he tells me to accept as freely and as innocently as a child free in the springtime? Why should I fear the ceasing of words when it was not I but the Spirit who caused their appearance?

O Father, make me as free, as trusting, and as pliant as the tall sycamore swaying gently in the caressing wind! Standing there on the creek bank, its roots exposed by years of springtime flooding, it offers me its gift of hope. Help me to remember it when my own floods come. Or when the soft breezes of the Spirit become gales of sorrow or pain.

It is beautiful here. No sound but the busy scurrying of last year's leaves as they tumble and dance before the wind. The trees, bare of leaves, create their own beauty as each stands in the uniqueness of its construction.

And through it all flows the living water. The soft sound of its voice soothes my mind and stills my soul. And I rise renewed. Was it so with you, Jesus? Is that why you withdrew to those wilderness mountains?

On Being Born Again

*My mind contracts.
My senses tighten,
and I am thrust forward;
propelled into new birth.
The self within groans
to be born;
struggles to free itself
from the clinging bands
of fetal security.*

*Vainly I shrink back from knowing;
blindly brush aside
the blurred images
of a new beginning.*

*Torn between helpless rage
and burning curiosity,
I walk the limbo
of each day's necessity.*

*Their brave words mock me.
Their success bodes only
my failure.
They are aliens in my world.*

*No matter that others
have stood here, before me.
Each birth is isolated
in its terror and expectation.*

*Wait for me!
I'm coming!*

Music

I remember walking alone along dusty paths through the fields in summer twilight with the soft afterglow making silhouettes of buildings and trees. The wonder and fullness of such quiet beauty would make me desperate with the need to capture and express it. As a child, the only way it could be expressed was to sing, loud and free, with no one to hear but God and the shaggy dog who faithfully accompanied me. The words didn't matter so much then. They could as easily be a rowdy ballad as a hymn. But they released my spirit which soared away to touch the face of God as a child touches the face of a parent in love and wonder.

To touch God. To touch. To end the separation of myself from the world of wonder that surrounded me. But it was never enough just to touch. I could touch a tree. I could even hold my hand in the rain and touch the sky. No, not enough just to touch. I know now that the restless yearning was to be touched back.

To be touched. To be responded to. An intense child, silent, stubborn, and withdrawn, I did not know how to ask for touching. And so I sang. And was touched by the gentle wind of summer; by the silent touch of a cold nose on my hand; by the simple beauty of an Indiana farm and the wonder of God.

But not by people. I was suspicious of people. Born a twin and youngest by five years of eight children, I was always too young to be useful. So, feeling the lack of a place for myself in the fabric of that big busy family, I withdrew into a fantasy world, building elaborate "ranches" among the tree roots, using marbles for horses and people I could control, and drawing pictures on endless yellow tablets. I stayed on the side lines and watched and listened and wondered. And hungered to be a part of the big bustling world around me.

Music somehow reflected those yearnings. In the swelling of a symphony or the mellow note of a single instrument sang the hunger, the wonder, the longing I could not express. And I could be one with that. I could be touched by it. And for those few moments I could be whole.

The Poet

For me to hear my own work read is to view that work in an entirely new dimension. To struggle with an idea, a life situation, is to feel emotion. But in the writing and the mechanics of creation, the emotion is released, and the words sometimes lose their power to move me.

Then, one day I heard my words read by another. Suddenly the power was once more within them and the emotion lived again. Startled, I reacted like those around me. Except, this was my inner self that was being seen!

"Stop!" I wanted to cry. "I didn't know what it said!"

Pilgrim
(lyric)

I searched the sky to find the proof of God;
and there I saw a million galaxies.
But they were cold and spoke no word to me.
I bowed my head and turned to seek again.

I watched the hawk and the dove upon the wing.
I saw them soar in the wind so wild and free.
But the hawk swooped down, and the dove became his prey.
I bowed my head and turned to seek again.

For I was lost and wandered in the night.
I could not find an anchor for my soul.
Was there no way to fill the emptiness within?
Did no one care for a soul in pain?

I turned again and sought to find the way.
This time the path led to the mind of man.
I found we all believed our way to be the best.
I bowed my head and turned to seek again.

And then I saw the Man of Galilee.
And I knew the proof of God was in his smile.
The arms of Christ, outstretched to all the world,
to hold us close within the heart of God!

Seeker & Scribe

Questing

I look back over the years of my seeking and know that for every valley filled with questions, there have been mountaintops on which the answers filled my mind and heart with such awe that my mind hungered anew for more knowledge of a world so complex and a God so infinitely surprising. And the more that is revealed, the further away move the horizons until I know that the frontiers of knowledge will not be reached in this lifetime.

Questions. Hard questions that tug at the soul and demand an answer. Do you love me, God? Do you love me, world? Is life good? And the seeker searches until that day when God smiles upon him, takes his hand and shows him the truth—that the seeker has been found. And God rejoices in the finding!

Seeker

God, my world is out of balance,
   and the tension hurts.
Who am I?
What am I doing here?
Your word comes to me from every side,
   and I stand in confusion
   before this maelstrom of opportunity.

Can I not escape?
Can I not retreat into the safe anonymity
   of everyday necessity?
You say, "Speak,"
   when my tongue stammers to a halt.
You say, "Love,"
   as I shrink back into my portable shell.

Is this woman who lives in here,
Mother?
Wife?
Daughter?
Or is she
Christian?
Seeker?
Leader?

"The same skin can hold them both," you say.
Ridiculous!

Who can concentrate on seeking
   with an eye full of oatmeal
   and a lapful of squirming humanity?
Who do I lead with no formal training,
   no background of "correct" requirements?

"Play it by ear!"
Have I the right?
Isn't there danger of misleading those who follow?
O God! I can think of so many excuses!

But the word is still there.
It will not let me go.
It fills my life.
It invades my world.
I am surprised by love
   and compelled by joy to speak.

So be it!
I am woman.
I am Christian.
I am seeker!
But best of all, Father
   I am your beloved child!

Church

How easy it is to fall into routine. Our lives become comfortable; they seem to progress through all the correct stages. And we become suspicious of any change. There are distant echoes of a restless searching, but they are more and more easily dismissed. Until we find ourselves going mechanically through life, unthinking, uncaring.

But once we realize this state of affairs exists, we must make a choice—either to give up that spark of independence, that deep knowledge of our ability to make our own contribution to the world around us, or to stand squarely against a deadening lethargy which seeks to suck us into the quicksand of indifference.

The sheer volume of communication in today's world can bring about or hasten this indifference rather than combat it. We are flooded with words and ideas continually until we no longer hear them. We "tune them out" in defense of our sanity. Mass communication has brought crises to our attention from every corner of the globe. A street fight in Hong Kong is emblazoned on the evening news as though our very lives depended on its outcome; as though every problem, every catastrophe, every disagreement somehow must be decided upon and acted upon by *us*. And, as we are confronted by all these crisis situations, we turn away and find our own personal world changing around us. So, we fear any deviation from routine that might seem to precipitate us into the dizzying rat race of the mass media world.

Part of us wants church to be more relevant, more supportive and meaningful, and part of us wants it to remain unchanged, foursquare, world without end. So we sit in worship services and fidget. We sit in board meetings and quibble. We take one step forward and one backward. At times we ponder; at other times we sit lethargically and let the world boil around our quiet backwater. But the ediface is leaking. The world's storms roar closer. Our children demand answers and turn restless eyes upon our pious posturings. The church must awake. Could it be that the Spirit is shaking that sleeping giant that she might come into her full potential for service?

Discovery

God, you said, "Love me!"
And I tried, I really did.
I went to church, and I prayed.
I used all the right words
  at all the right times.
And you know, I almost
  had myself believing it.

But, it seemed the more I did,
  the more I had to do.
Just to be sure.
Because I didn't really feel
  anything.
Not inside, where I lived.
If you really want to know,
  it felt more like hate.

"Love me, or go to hell!"
I'm sorry, God,
  but that's the way it sounded.
And I almost left,
  because I couldn't love
  a God like that.

But where else was there?
Who else had the answers?
So, I took a second look,
  just to make sure you were
  a monster!

Well, you know the rest.
Almost like you had it planned!
Who would have known the path of doubt
  would lead me back to you?
Now I know who loved first.
Now I know who loves freely.

*For the first time
   I can smile with my heart,
   and not just my mouth.
I see you, God, not in church,
   but in people.
Sure, I go to church;
   but now I take you with me!*

*And when the preacher gets too
   super-pious,
I look him in the eye
   and I think,
   "Throw him a little doubt, God,
   it's good for what ails him!"*

Leaders

Are some of us leaders because we are afraid to be askers . . . followers . . . beggars? Do we give to cover our own want? Is our leading an escape from loneliness, and do we speak the word of hope from within the pain of hopelessness?

Who counsels the counselor? Who comforts the comforter? Will the time ever come when we can accept love and affirmation as our natural right instead of being forever and uncomfortably surprised by it? From whom do we dare to ask a blessing, to say, "Even as I grow, part of me is dying because I cannot accept God's love for me. His love for others, maybe, but not for me!"

Tradition says the answer is God. And we know that is ultimately true. But what of those times when we ache for a touch, a word that we can both feel and hear? Dare we look to those we lead? Dare we turn off that neon facade of pretty lights and gracious invitations to continue the lie that all is well with fearless leader? Would they understand?

Searching Heart

*They look at me as though I had
   an answer, God.
They look to me for leadership
   and instruction.*

*How do I tell them I also am
   a pilgrim?
How do I convince them
   I have no easy answers?*

*Would they understand these dark
   nights of despair?
Would they understand the agony
   of daily failures?
This endless, restless searching
   for life's secrets?*

*My soul finds no rest
   within safe walls.
And I fear the danger
   of leading them astray.*

*Guard my tongue as I speak, God,
   and keep my searching heart
   safe in your own.*

Christian Complacency

I sit here, smug in my
 Christian complacency.
Let the preacher rant and rave . . .
 at my neighbor.

I'm safe.
I feel no sinful pleasure.
I feel no animosity.
Of course,
 I don't feel much of anything else,
 either.

So I sit here;
 placid,
 unfeeling,
 sleepy,
 uninterested.
Let the preacher preach.
I'll even pay him to do it.
Only make it loud,
 so I can't hear God!

And No Song Rose to Heaven

*And the waves rolled on
  over the face of the deep.
Dark and cold were the waters;
  lonely and wide was the sky.*

*And the waves swept on so tall
  there appeared to be no sky.
For all the elements mingled there
  in wild and primeval chaos.*

*And no thing breathed.
And no one loved.
And no song rose to heaven.*

*Then, slowly spread across the restless deep
  a Presence.
And closer the Presence came
  until it hovered over the sea.*

*And in that Presence brooded
  an awesome intellect.
And from that Presence came forth such power
  as to still the chaotic sea.*

*The waves stilled and became
  a gentle lapping upon the shores of time.
A great voice, like the sound
  of many waters, spoke,*

*"Let there be light!"
and it was so.*

*But no thing breathed.
And no one loved.
And no song rose to heaven.*

*The primeval chaos became
  a green and fertile earth
  as fragrant grasses and stately trees
  clothed the hills and rimmed the quiet waters.*

The seasons waxed and waned.
The vastness of the universe twinkled
with the dust of a billion stars.
Warm, golden day was followed
by the moon-silvered night.

But still no thing breathed.
And no one loved.
But a song rose to heaven.

Yes, the whisper of the wind,
the sighings of the grass,
and the clear babble of the brook.

Then, at the command of the Creator,
there appeared life upon the earth;
of infinite variety and in perfect order;
Each in its place, each in its time.

And now there was breath upon the earth,
and the singing of birds and living things.
But still, no one loved.

Therefore, in the midst of an ordered universe,
the Presence that had brooded over the primeval deep
stooped down into the dust of a world
and shaped a new being.

Knowing full well this new entity
could one day deny and reject its very Creator,
God placed humanity upon the stage of history.

And the wonder within us
matched the wonder of our God.
And we breathed.
And we loved.
And we sang of creation.
And we loved the creation.
And we forgot the Creator.

The Babies

The babies are trying
  to tell us something.
They are restless and fretful.
They know better than to sit in
  a stuffy church building
  and be yelled at.

I sometimes wish I were a baby again,
  so I could voice my own complaint.
What do they think of us,
  as we sit here half asleep;
  spiritually quiescent?

Do they feel our restlessness?
The impatience that lies so near
  this silent surface?
Are they expressing our dissatisfaction?

More power to 'em,
  let 'em yell!

I Wondered

I wondered where all the love had gone.
I wondered why no one seemed to care.
I looked in vain for one or two
    who really saw people.

"Is your world going so wrong?"
I asked God.

Then I looked inward
    and saw hate masquerading
    as righteous indignation.
I saw callous indifference
    shrugging beneath my "uninvolvement."

I saw apathy and self-interest.
I saw my own soul.
And I knew.
God forgive me!
I knew!

The Stream

I saw the thing
  and thought it wept.
Oh, there are no tears, I said.
Things have no tears.
They cannot weep.

Then, I remembered how God had made it,
  such a lovely quiet stream;
  cool
  and singing through the living land.

And I wept for it.
To see the filth and scum
  sliding, bumping,
  brushing over the rocks
  like some obscene lover,
  leaving a gift of rancid fragrance
  to mingle with the offerings
  of my brothers and sisters.

And the stream flows on
  with no one to watch it die
  but God
  who stands on the bank
  weeping for his children.

They

They said:
> Put your trust in God.
> Follow his rules.
> Live by Christ's word.
> Get saved.
> Go to church.
> Have faith!

I asked:
> Who is God?
> Won't you show him to me?
> Is he real to you?
> Does he love you?
> Does he love me?
> Do you love me?

They answered:
> Read the Bible.
> Pray a lot.
> But don't ask questions!

Planting Vineyards

*If you would be friend to me
  don't say, "I love you."
Don't call me special or unique.
Just take the time to know me.*

*I need your love
  and affirmation too much
  to clutch at the straw of words.*

*How easily words flow
  in this new Christianity!
Everyone loves everyone.
The whole world
  is the whole world's lover.*

*But I'm not the whole world.
I am myself, and I don't know
who I am anymore.
If I ever did.*

*I don't want your promiscuous loving.
Give that to the faceless world.*

*But could we take the time
  to be friends?
Is there time enough for that
  in this era of instant brotherhood?*

*Do you have the time
  before rushing off to the next conquest?*

*It must be terribly important
  to save the world
  if we can't stop to plant vineyards.*

Home Again

God,
    I looked for you and thought you were gone.
The others felt you;
    at least they said they did.
They said you were easy to find . . .
    and turned again to their devotions.

I looked some more.
I read the Bible and found evidence
    of a God who loved people.
And I tried again to reach you.

But for all my reaching,
    you were still absent.
In despair I turned from reaching.
And, as I turned, I caught a glimpse of you.
Caught in the eyes of those around me
    were flickers of a new being.

Slowly, so slowly I move toward you.
And, with a burst of joy,
    I see you running to meet me!
I see the love in your eyes,
    the compassion of your touch.

As I hold the hand of my brother
    I feel yours.
As I hear the words of my sister
    I hear yours.
Their arms are yours;
    their love and acceptance reflects
    your approval of me.

And now I know, Father.
You are not standing far off in your Heaven.
You did not quit speaking to us.
You are speaking.
You are acting.
You are loving, moving, confronting.

It's good to be home, Father!

His Touch Within
(lyric)

You say God is in his heaven,
   but what does that mean to me?
I cannot touch his face
   or plumb the mystery!
I am bound within this crystal ball
   of earth and sky and sea.
It's beauty pleases me.
No other do I see!

And if beauty were not marred by pain,
   I'd never look away.
I'd live my life and then
   be one with earth again.
Ah, but something deep within my soul
   will not be stilled, my friend.
It says there must be more
   to spend my living for!

You see, perfection finds an echo
   in the musings of my mind.
To miss the greater plan
   I'd have to travel blind.
From the softness of a baby's smile
   to the loneliness of death;
Our paths are crossed by him.
He touches every breath!

Still, it's true I do not see
   but his touch remains within.
He fills my mind!
And calls me back to him!

My Father's Garden

Down wind-swept summer hills I ran;
   barefoot, on trails cut deep by patient sheep
   and bumptious goats.
Sun-warmed earth and fragrant grass
   were my pillow
   as I contemplated the vault of heaven.

My spirit soared with the eagle
   and my sturdy boy's legs
   strained after the bounding deer.

Oh, how I loved my Father's garden.
I loved my Father's garden!
I roamed my Father's garden
   in those dusty boyhood days.

From village streets I wandered
   to cities full and rank.
I saw the twisted, tortured lives
   and the weary, empty journeyings.

Gone was the clean, bracing smell
   of summer hillsides.
Gone the carefree days of youth.
But the fragrance of souls was heady wine
   and their minds were sweet to me as wild honey.

I loved my Father's garden.
I loved my Father's garden!
I healed their souls in my Father's garden
   when manhood came my way.

They hung me in His garden,
   on one of His anguished trees.
I could feel its aching shame
   as it submitted to the will of man.

The summer hills blurred.
My spirit sought the eagle.
My weary eyes fell upon the people.
Their minds are still my honey,
  their souls my wine.

Oh, I loved my Father's garden.
I loved my Father's garden!
I watered my Father's garden
  with my life's blood and my tears.

Now, when I see a sun-browned,
  lean-limbed youth
  bursting over summer hills;
When I see his gaze captured by eagle and deer,
  my heart overflows with memory.
And I am once more in a garden
  newborn, released, fulfilled.

As my brothers come to me
  from walking in my Father's garden,
  I point to earth and say,

"I love my Father's garden.
My Father's fruitful garden!
I was seed for my Father's garden,
  and you are the golden grain!"

Woman & Wayfarer

John

John loves his life's work. He was born to work the soil and manhandle those huge tractors and gentle the livestock. He is the most wonderfully natural man I've ever known, and he sometimes cannot understand my restlessness and my inability to be happy just being a housewife. He acknowledges my skill with words and pattern but doesn't seem to understand my need to create in my own way just as he does in his. In the meantime, he puts up with the crazy poet he married, who loves wild teenagers and doesn't bake him half enough pies.

And I thank God for sending me a mate who is such a beloved and respected man in the community and the ideal man for our children to look to as a father and example. He is as basic as the seasons. I am not. If it were not for John I would fly off in all directions at once. As I look back over our marriage, I see that we balance each other. The rich soil of his steadfastness permits me to flower and grow at a slow and steady pace. I think without him I would have become more like the wind poppies—bright but brief—instead of like the sturdy redbud tree we planted by the house when we were first married. It had grown steadily but slowly through the years of our marriage and only bloomed after sóme fifteen years. But in those first fragile blooms lay the promise of a continuing delight. I have hungered for quick success in everything I've ever attempted, and if I had had a husband who pushed me ahead, encouraging me in everything I tried, I would not have been forced to struggle and grow deep roots.

On the other hand, I think John will admit that I have added a new dimension to his life and shaken up a few of his preconceptions. What better gift could God give to a marriage than mutual admiration?

Interlude

*The night grows cold.
The blanket slips away
   and drowsily I seek you
   to share your warmth.*

*Let others write of the fire
   of passion's height,
I would speak now
   of gentler things—*

*The warmth of your
   strong body,
   the reassuring sound
   of your heartbeat;*

*The song in the night
   sung from a heart
   filled with wonder
   of touching you.*

*I rest in your silence,
   and the steady pulse
   of your integrity,
   your quiet caring.*

*My mind brushes against
   the mystery of your otherness
   even as I lie within
   the familiar curve of your arms.*

*Just a moment out of many,
   an interlude in one of many nights.
But one moment is enough for wonder,
and God is always there to hear my
   "Thank you!"*

Thoughts on a Winter's Eve

Like the silent snow
   my thoughts seek yours.
From its frozen shell
   my spirit mourns its mate.

Passion's fire burns dim and cold,
   and love's first song stands mute
before my lonely citadel.

Seeking to possess,
   I drive you from me.
Longing to give,
   I am bound by frustration and despair.

A lonely touching
   and silent parting.
Oh, that spirit could couple
   as easily as flesh!

Reach Out

Reach out!
Take my hand.
Hold it warm in your own.
Share with me your humanity.

My heart is so alone.
I search your eyes and see,
　mirrored there,
　a kindred loneliness.

Where is the bridge?
What path must we walk
　to meet in simple faith;
　to love as children, unafraid?

Reach out.
Take my hand.
Find the path with me.
Share my humanity.

Fear

Fear is that blind, unreasoning dread that we are ultimately alone in the universe. Thrust from the security of the womb into an unknown, untested vacuum, we are immediately bombarded with the fact of our separate being. We encounter rejection in disapproval, discipline, and sibling rivalry, and the fear grows. We become aware of the impermanence of relationships as death becomes real to us through the loss of a pet, stories of dying, or the loss of a significant person. If we cannot count on the security of our relationships or our place in the scheme of the world, we are lost.

Added to this is the child's primitive fear of God. No matter how lovingly we are confronted with our Sunday school God, we must inevitably come to grips with the fact of God's wrath. Even if it is played down, or explained to us, it does not disappear, but remains to surface again as doubt when we reach early adulthood. We may never realize that we really fear being alone in a universe that may be alien to us. If God is capable of turning away from us; if we someday could find ourselves bereft of any comfort or love, we must live the rest of our lives in a low-key hysteria, blindly cramming our lives with pacifiers in order not to think of the void beyond. Nameless fears and phobias are clung to unconsciously in hopes the real threat may somehow be dealt with.

This is why God is the only answer to ultimate fear. When we can know the truth that is God, we will know his love is incapable of being ended. We will know that we are not alone in a cold and aimless universe, or in the sway of a vengeful God. When this is perceived in the deepest core of our being, peace floods our world and makes it habitable for the human soul. As a child flees out of darkness into the light and warmth of a mother's arms, so do we rush into the arms of the all mighty, all powerful, and all loving God. And fear is lost in peace.

Alone

I am alone in the night.
My mind centers down tight and still.
I am alone.
Who will care if I hurt?
Who will weep if I die?

They are almost gone
  who loved me.
Almost all.
And those few who remain will,
  one by one,
  disappear into that terrible void.

I am alone in the night.
And my heart strives to bind itself
  into a stone of uncaring indifference.
I do not need this world that does not care!

Don't reach out.
Don't touch the void.
Don't look up and see the empty sky.
Don't pray to that vengeful God

Who takes and takes
  'til I have nothing.
And, laughing, takes himself away
  with the rest!

Don't tell me I'm wrong!
Your empty lives underline my bitter thoughts.
And I find no comfort in your vague posturings.

I am alone in the night.
The faith that once touched the face of God
  has fallen in the storm of contemporary reason,
  and I must cower before its scientific answers.

Oh, if God were real!
If only he made a difference in your life!
Maybe then I could trust him with mine
   and not be alone.

Don't leave me!

Stolen Moments

Visiting hours were over.
I tried not to be impatient,
  but the atmosphere here always depressed me.
So with exaggerated patience I waited for my friend
  on the small side porch.

They didn't see me standing by the far railing.
Their eyes were dim and misty,
  and if they noticed me at all it was to suppose
  me another old one.
He used a cane,
  she a walker,
  and their steps were slow and trembling.
The door gave them trouble
  and I started to help,
  but they managed it and were at last outside.

She was frail and brittle-looking
  like an old lace valentine;
  he was stooped and thin.
They'd come through the door apart,
  but now I saw him take her hand,
  as they stood there looking into the gathering dusk.
For many moments they were silent
  as though privacy were too precious to be wasted.
Then I saw their lips move
  and heard snatches of sound.

I thought of slipping back into the building,
  for I felt an intruder here.
But just then a starched attendant came bustling
  through the door.
"I thought I'd find you here!
Don't you know it's getting chilly?
Naughty of you two to run off like this!
Now, let's get back to your warm room!"

*As she herded them back through the door,
  she caught my eye with a conspiratorial air.
And I remembered the room I had left with relief
  a short time ago.
The supervisor had been so accommodating and helpful
  when he said they could share a room here.
After all, after sixty years it would be heartless to
  separate them.
Too bad they were so old and worn out.
So sadly senile.
Too bad our modern homes were too crowded to accommodate
  the old folks.*

*They must be better off here.
Better care.
Constant supervision.
If only their words had been less distinguishable.*

"Yea though we walk through the valley of the shadow . . .
I love you, Margaret. . . ."
"I love you, Tom."

Reflections on "Minnie Remembers"

"Why did you write 'Minnie Remembers'? Was there a real Hank and a real Minnie?" Many have asked me these questions. Yes, there was a real Minnie, and there was a real Hank. They were my paternal grandparents, and Hank did precede Minnie in death by twenty years or so. But I don't know if Minnie ever really had thoughts like these. You see, Minnie lived with us all through the years of my childhood. But I accepted her as part of the furniture of my life; the way I accepted the foreverness of life; the way I accepted the uncomplicated God of Sunday school; the way I accepted the invulnerability and perfection of my parents.

Yes, there was a Minnie, but I did not know her.

It was not until I learned of loneliness myself that I knew Minnie. I did not consciously write "Minnie Remembers" as an answer to my own loneliness. I did not write it as an exercise or with the expectation of having it printed and reprinted hundreds of times. No poet does that. "Minnie Remembers" came out of a cauldron of feelings and memories that was bubbling and boiling deep inside.

One of those memories was of a story I read fifteen or twenty years ago in a women's magazine about an old lady who was dying of a stroke. Her daughter sat by her bed and tried to understand what her mother wanted when she looked at her so pleadingly. The mother could not speak, but her eyes eloquently portrayed some need deep inside. Almost at the last, the daughter happened to glance at a paper laying nearby with her mother's name on it. Suddenly realizing why her mother's eyes had been pleading so, the daughter leaned close and whispered, "Hello, Alice Marie Smith! You are a beautiful person, Alice, and I love you!"

A beautiful smile spread over her mother's face and she relaxed against the pillows. I'm sure I have not done justice to the real story and cannot even quote the name of it, but I've never forgotten the lesson it taught. That was the germ of "Minnie Remembers" the realization that we are all individuals with identities, and those identities are precious to us; that our names become so imbued with the essence of ourselves that to hear them is to be reminded of our own presence in the world.

    Yes, there is a Minnie. She sits in a thousand, a million rooms in America. She remembers. She wonders if anyone will speak her name. She longs for the touch of compassion, of companionship and love. She wonders why God has given her life without meaning. She waits, and she remembers.

Minnie Remembers

God,
my hands are old.
I've never said that out loud before
but they are.
I was so proud of them once.
They were soft
like the velvet smoothness of a firm, ripe
peach.
Now the softness is more like worn-out sheets
or withered leaves.
When did these slender, graceful hands
become gnarled, shrunken claws?
When, God?
They lie here in my lap,
naked reminders of this worn-out
body that has served me too well.

How long has it been since someone touched me?
Twenty years?
Twenty years I've been a widow.
Respected.
Smiled at.
But never touched.
Never held so close that loneliness
was blotted out.

I remember how my mother used to hold me,
God.
When I was hurt in spirit or flesh,
she would gather me close,
stroke my silky hair,
and caress my back with her warm hands.
O God, I'm so lonely!

I remember the first boy who ever kissed me.
We were both so new at that!
The taste of young lips and popcorn,
the feeling inside of mysteries to come.

WOMAN AND WAYFARER

I remember Hank and the babies.
How else can I remember them but together?
Out of the fumbling, awkward attempts of new lovers
came the babies.
And as they grew, so did our love.
And, God, Hank didn't seem to mind
if my body thickened and faded a little.
He still loved it.
And touched it.
And we didn't mind if we were no longer beautiful.
And it felt so good.
And the children hugged me a lot.
O God, I'm lonely!

God, why didn't we raise the kids to be silly
and affectionate as well as
dignified and proper?
You see, they do their duty.
They drive up in their fine cars;
they come to my room to pay their respects.
They chatter brightly and reminisce.
But they don't touch me.
They call me "Mom" or "Mother"
or "Grandma."

Never Minnie.
My mother called me Minnie.
So did my friends.
Hank called me Minnie, too.
But they're gone.
And so is Minnie.
Only Grandma is here.
And God! She's lonely!

Travail

Spring sketches bold charcoal patterns
  against the rose-hued west.

Robins whisper their evening song
  above the silent profusion
    of life awakening.

Hope strives deep within
  to rise with the quickening
    flow of God's world.

But the frost of winter,
  silver-tipped with the currency of despair
    works with icy fingers;
      tamping hope deeper within heart's prison.

Come soon, summer sun,
  warm this landlocked soul
    and send it heavenward!

Beginning Again

Beginning again. How many times throughout our lives have we come to the land of beginning again? A land of sorrow and defeat—a place where our plans and dreams seem miles from completion as we stand amid the broken pieces of life.

We look at those things we must lay aside. Some of the work was good and so lovingly done, and we hope it will not have been entirely in vain.

Are we diminished for having failed? Or is it possible that God uses our failures as the darker thread in his tapestry?

Still, we stand perplexed, feeling lost and alone; wanting to pull our tattered pride around us and withdraw from the battle. But life is waiting. There are things to be done, people to care for. And God is there.

Before we even think to call, even before we turn blindly toward the light and warmth of his love, God is there. And, laying aside our defeats we once again press on toward the prize of the high calling of God.

On the Loss of a Son

Bone of my bone
and flesh of my flesh;
yet now you stand before me a stranger;
one who has become an alien,
an outcast seeking refuge
in the ground of memory.

"My son!
My heart cries out to you!"

But my mind rules
as it has ever done.
Until I drive you into a bitter retreat.

Do you know my heart is breaking
as I see the hurt,
the pleading in your eyes?
Can you know the tearing anguish
that threatens to destroy
reason and law?

Are you somehow aware
that I stand guard
before the sanctity of moral order?
That I am pledged to punish you
by withholding my love and approval
as I did when you were in my shadow?

I bent the twig as best I could
and pruned and tended
the tender vine of your will
until you bore fruit.

But, your fruit is bitter!
Sorrow and brokenness
are a wall between my garden and yours,
and I dare not let you in.

*In my mind I call to you,
run to you,
gather you close and comfort you.
But I turn away, and I am bereft,
as though flesh and bone
were diminished and age increased.
Cold and lonely,
I watch you walk away.*

Masks

I'm not sure whether we learn to take off our masks, or whether they just wear out with age. Perhaps we finally live long enough to realize they don't work, or that we no longer need them much. Maybe we tire of being thought helpless or strong or all wise. Or maybe we realize we haven't really fooled anyone, and if our family and friends like us, they do so in spite of our foolishness.

So, like a child playing peek-a-boo, we drop our mask for a moment. And the sky does not fall. It just gets a little bigger, a little brighter. So, we try another peek. And so it goes until the realization hits us that we are almost free! And we look people in the eye as equals. And we see them better. And their masks no longer bother us.

Then, one day, we begin to see others peek out from behind their masks. And we're ready to welcome them into the sunshine!

Word vs. Touch

Our words are there.
They fill the room between us.
Dropping into the silence
  they analyze and explain.

Kind words, wise words;
  the dialogue of enlightened men.
Our words are ripples of concentric circles;
  words touching words.

But the Word became flesh
  and dwelt among us.
And touched us.
His words challenged and taught.
But his touch healed.

Words can become walls, built slowly,
  syllable by syllable;
  shutting you out, shutting me in.
Leaving us cold.

Pardon me, sir,
  for interrupting your conversation.
But would you please stop talking
  and touch me?

Facade

Sometimes,
  if I could just cry, Jesus.
Sometimes
  if I could just cry!

This painted smile
  I hide behind;
Plastered to my soul
  like flypaper.

Covering my fears,
  my insecurity;
blocking my joy
  with its schizophrenic hypocrisy!

People come to me
  for help, Jesus.
They see my cardboard smile,
  and come.

I try not to disappoint
  them.
But do they know?
  Do they see?

Does this facade
  of dignity
wear thin
  upon closer inspection?

If I could just cry,
  sometimes, Jesus.
If I could just cry!

Broken Wall

Hey, out there!
Do you see?
There's a hole in my wall!

It's not very big,
  and it's in kind of an out of the way spot.
But it's there.
And if you've got the time,
  and work at it,
  maybe you could make it bigger.

You see, lately, I've noticed
  that it's kind of lonely in here
  all by myself.
And I've begun to wonder what it would be like
  out there in the open
  where you are.

Do you care?
Would I be welcome out there?
Is that love I feel drifting in?
Is that warmth flowing through the hole in my wall?

Maybe I could work at it from this side, too.

Did You Ever Cry, Jesus?

Did you ever cry, Jesus?
did the world ever pile up on you
  'til you wanted to quit?

Did you ever cry, Jesus?
Did you ever get so tired of humanity
  you wished you'd never come?

Did life ever throw you too much hate?
Were there more lies and apathy
  than could be borne silently?

Did your back ever ache, Jesus?
Did you sometimes fret at family obligations
  and long to be about your Father's business?

Did the blind eyes, the twisted bodies,
the warped minds and maimed souls get to you?
  Were you ever just plain mad?

Were you ever lonely, Jesus?
When your friends misunderstood and walked out on you,
  did you ever cry, Jesus?

I think you must have,
for you know me so well. So well!
  I think you must have cried a little.

Windows of the Soul

The eyes of a child hold the mysteries of God.
They draw our gaze irresistibly to their depths,
  there to catch us unaware with the breathlessness of
  spring.

Decadence recoils from the clear-eyed glance of a child.
Hearts are broken by the lost bewilderment in the eyes
  of an unloved waif.
The battle-hardened soldier beholds the atrocities
  of war reflected in the eyes of an emaciated babe,
  and drawing it to himself,
  damns all wars.

The eyes of a child hold the mysteries of God.
Mothers bathe their souls in it and become wise.
Fathers consider their goals by the light of its
  effervescent optimism, and grow to meet it.

God looks into the eyes of a child
  and declares his creation to be very good.
God watches the clear, untouched panes become dulled
  with disillusionment;
  growing dark and evasive as sin clouds them year by
  year, and God weeps.

Soul on Tiptoe

They don't understand me, God.
And I don't know how to tell them,
for I don't understand either.

My spirit leaps upward
and runs on feet so light
they must surely dance on the North Star
and leave Earth weeping below!

My heart sings
with wordless tongue so beautiful
I fear it will burst with singing!

New worlds appear.
New rhythms dance within me,
and I would be away!
Away!

Away . . .
Where am I bound?
What far country beckons?
What is this new song,
this rhythm within?

My soul stands on tiptoe
as, hands uplifted to tomorrow,
I turn again to yesterday.

I see a place where love is free
and laughter echoes back to me.
A place I knew so well
and never thought to leave.
Warmth
Laughter
Love
and singing trees.

But I must be away!
Soft winds call
and I cannot stay.

Oh, weep for me, curly-headed dolls!
Cry for the little girl
  with jelly-flavored kisses
  who will march no more to the fairy band.

She's going away, you see.
Yes, she's forgotten you.
She must fly from misty-eyed mothers
  and safe harbors.

Ah, but don't weep too long
  for I am bound from love to love;
  and if the bridge on which I stand
  seems weak and fearsome,
  still I must cross it.

But lightly,
  so lightly!
For my spirit soars
  and I must be away!
Trembling to the rhythm within
  I turn to tomorrow.

The End and the Beginning

What does the future hold? In the act of writing this book, I have broken the shell of my isolation. As I venture into the editorial offices of The Upper Room, I initiate new relationships and dare seek new horizons.

The pages of this book speak of a song sung in the isolation of a lonely searching; a restless seeking for relationships with those around me. Will the poetry continue? Or will it cease now that my silence has been broken?

This has been a real fear in the past months.

Some of the most feeling poetry has come from my struggle with depression and the search for wholeness. And the question keeps coming back. Will I be able to praise God with the same power that characterized my battles with him as the Holy Adversary? Having found a way to bring beauty out of a life situation, will I find the courage to move from that situation to a new one?

However, in looking through files and drawers seeking information for the book, I come across words and poems scribbled on church bulletins and old envelopes. Words such as "Earth Song" and "Discovery." And I realize there will always be words. Words for the times when life seems so full of joy and promise that only song will free my spirit to breathe. For times when the wonder of a new friend or a new insight into God's love leaves me speechless and I must look deep within to find those singing words to tell you I love you.

Yes, the words are there. And the seeing, the feeling, the knowing. As long as others hurt and struggle with life, I will feel with them that isolation, that desperate need to know and be known. And, God willing, I will touch them. I will say to them, "I know you hurt. I know you struggle behind the barricades of your failures and your mute seeking for love and affirmation." And, out of my own seeking, I can say more, "I know God will find you! I know he will not let you go if you will give him what is yours to give. He will give you love beyond your mute imaginings. And affirm the specifically unique person he created you to be!" I can say from experience, "God loves you!"

My time of reaching has given me long arms to wrap around my world. The loving affirmation I have received from God and from those who believed in me has filled my heart to overflowing with love enough to share with you. And doubt has confirmed my faith.

Now I can do no more than give to God the gift of self that was his creation and ask him to use it to his glory.

Index of Titles

Alone   74
And No Song Rose to
   Heaven   56
Babies, The   58
Beginning Again   83
Broken Wall   89
Challenge   29
Christian Complacency   55
Church   50
Dichotomy   24
Did You Ever Cry, Jesus?   90
Discovery   51
Earth Song   30
Empty Spaces   35
End and the Beginning,
   The   94
Facade   88
Fear   73
Flight   27
Freedom   26
Friend   37
Healing   34
His Touch Within   64
Hollow Place   32
Home Again   63
Interlude   70
In the Woods   39
I Wondered   59
John   69
Joy   31

Leaders   53
Little Turtle   25
Masks   86
Mind Song   19
Minnie Remembers   80
Music   41
My Father's Garden   65
On Being Born Again   40
On the Loss of a Son   84
Pilgrim   43
Pine, The   33
Planting Vineyards   62
Poet, The   42
Questing   47
Reach Out   72
Reflections on "Minnie
   Remembers"   78
Searching Heart   54
Seeker   48
Solace   36
Soul on Tiptoe   92
Stolen Moments   76
Stream, The   60
They   61
Thoughts on a Winter's Eve   71
To Be One   22
Travail   82
Windows of the Soul   91
Words   21
Word vs. Touch   87